The Lucky 7 Lessons

They Don't Teach You at Princeton, Yale, and Harvard

Melvin (Mel) Masuda

The Lucky 7 Lessons

They Don't Teach You at Princeton, Yale, and Harvard

Melvin (Mel) Masuda

LEGACY ISLE
PUBLISHING

ISBN 978-1-948011-65-5

Design and production
Ingrid Lynch

Legacy Isle Publishing
1000 Bishop St., Ste. 806
Honolulu, HI 96813
Telephone 1-808-587-7766
Toll-free 1-866-900-BOOK
info@legacyislepublishing.net
www.legacyislepublishing.net

Printed in the United States

Contents

Dedicated to...

Son Maka, Iolani School Class of 1998;
daughter-in-law Allison (nee Ayers); and
their fraternal twin sons, Ikaika and Kapono

and

Daughter Kaiewa (nee Masuda),
Kamehameha Schools-Kapalama, Class of 2001;
son-in-law Matthew (Matt); and
their sons, Kahiau and Keolaloa

Foreword

I am writing this book at, as the saying goes, the "ripe old age" of almost 80 (circa 2021). Looking back, I can hardly believe that I've been so lucky as to have earned—through scholarships, loans, and work-study jobs—degrees from Princeton, Yale, and Harvard, in that order. (A bachelor's degree from Princeton, *cum laude* (but it took me five years, not four—see Lucky Lesson #7); a Juris Doctor law degree from Yale Law School, where I had the honor of being chosen an editor of the *Yale Law Journal*; and a master's in public administration from Harvard Kennedy School, student body president.)

Looking back over the past generation and a half, I've realized that there are "7 lucky lessons" they don't teach you in the classrooms of Princeton, Yale, and Harvard.

Lucky Lesson #1

Contrary to novelist Thomas Wolfe's book title
***You Can't Go Home Again*, you have to decide for**
yourself—if you've left home for college and other
adventures—whether you really *want* to "go home
again" when, inevitably, the time arrives for you to
settle down permanently.

My classmates and friends from Yale Law School often ask me, via the Internet, "Why didn't you come to a Wall Street law firm like us?"

Having been born and raised in the Hawaiian Islands, I truly *wanted* to go home again. It was—and is—a deliberate choice. I had never been away from Hawaii before I left for Princeton in 1960. The lifestyle in the Islands as well as its beautiful tropical setting (what Mark Twain called "the loveliest fleet of Islands that lies anchored in any ocean") and its unique history (among other events, where World War II started for the USA with the Pearl Harbor attack) all drew me back—despite the high cost of living.

For others, the choice of where to settle down permanently has often gone the other way, away from their original home—and I respect that. We are all unique individuals, and we make our own decisions as to where and when we put down our permanent roots. As the time-honored French saying goes: *Chacun a son gout!* "To each, her or his own choice!"

Lucky Lesson #2

Outside the classroom, you're on your own in figuring out your sense of sexual ethics. Best of luck!

The #MeToo movement that emerged full force in 2017 verifies this lesson that you learn outside the classrooms of Princeton, Yale, and Harvard. I would hope that you arrive at the Golden Rule.

I just missed the boat of coeducation at Princeton, which graduated its first eight female undergraduates in 1970. I was the last of the "*ancien regime*," so to speak, in the early 1960s, when (believe it or not) young women from nearby colleges were bussed in to the Princeton gym for dance "mixers" once a month. As one who had attended coed public schools prior to Princeton, this ritual always struck me as odd. When I became a senior and was on the board of the student newspaper, the *Daily Princetonian*, we shocked the college administration by publishing a front page editorial urging coeducation.

Lucky Lesson #3

You learn pretty quickly that the intellectual life of Princeton, Yale, and Harvard is different from the "real world"—and that "never the twain shall meet."

The first summer I came home to Hawaii from Princeton, I got into a huge shouting match with my uncle (through marriage) who happened to be an American of Japanese ancestry (AJA). Although he had rarely ever met a Black person, he asserted that he "didn't like Negroes." As I would have in a small group discussion in my Princeton classes, I confronted him immediately: "How can you say that? You haven't had that much contact." (The few Blacks in Hawaii at that time, pre-Barack Obama, were military troops.) My uncle exploded: "How can you say that to me? Show more respect!"

Lesson learned: My idealistic notion of being unprejudiced— so acceptable in small group discussions at Princeton—had come up against the "real world"—and I had lost.

Lucky Lesson #4

As an individual of color, I always have to be prepared for the slings and arrows of subtle, micro-aggressive, stereotype-based statements; for acts of overt racism; and even, during the time of the COVID-19 pandemic, for being attacked physically.

In my freshman class of 800 at Princeton, I was one of only seven persons of color—five Asian Americans, one Black American, and one African prince. At Yale Law School, I was one of only two Asian Americans in my entering class of 120. And, at Harvard Kennedy School, I was again one of only two Asian Americans, this time in an entering class of 60.

But with my obviously Japanese physical features, I certainly stuck out in a crowd. To borrow an anachronistic latter-day image, I felt like the blue-skinned Disney space alien "Stitch," who crash-landed on Earth (on Kauai, of all places). (Nowadays, as I write this 20 years into the 21st century, Asian Americans comprise 15 percent of the entering class at Princeton. How times change!)

During my senior year at Princeton, as the Vietnam War was raging and US draftees were being sent to Southeast Asia, I attended a college conference at the Air Force Academy in Colorado Springs. After the conference, I was on a bus to Denver for my flight back East, when a GI began to verbally harass me, calling me "gook" off-and-on all the way to the airport. Fortunately, he didn't physically attack me, but no one on the bus came to my defense.

Incidents like this can happen even in polyglot Hawaii. During the COVID-19 pandemic, as a group of six slightly inebriated whites passed me on the street in downtown Honolulu, one of them shouted out to me, "Ching Chong, Chinaman!" Luckily, he didn't stop to beat me up.

So, you can understand why I am forever grateful to two white friends in particular—one from both Princeton and Yale, the other a Yalie—who took the time and made the effort to look past my stereotypical Asian physical features (skinny, five feet five inches, an obviously ethnic face) and, through long bull sessions, saw that our world views on issues and values were simpatico. Each of them—Reed Guthridge of Florida and Robbin (Rob) Johnson of Minnesota, who became a Rhodes Scholar after Yale—invited me to be a groomsman, the only one of color, at their respective wedding ceremonies back in the early 1970s. I'm sure that, even now in the 21st century, people looking at those wedding photos ask, "… And who's this Asian guy in the picture?"

Lucky Lesson #5

Growing up immigrant and working class isn't all that it's cracked up to be. Instead, I found it to be a rough-and-tumble upbringing, and I'm lucky I turned out okay.

My dad, Tatsuo, who went through only the eighth grade in Japan, emigrated from Namie village, Fukushima Prefecture, and reached US soil in the Territory of Hawaii in 1921. That was just before the immigration gate slammed shut, with the effective date of the US Japanese-And-All-Other-Asians Exclusion Act in 1924. (The US Chinese Exclusion Act had taken effect earlier, in 1882.)

Child labor laws weren't being enforced in the Territory, and Tatsuo was sent at age 13 to be a laborer in the sugar cane fields of Maui. He lucked out five years later when he was able to get an indoor job as a dining room waiter at the sugar plantation hotel. Maui had only 30,000 residents back then, with no resort hotels. Now, it's known worldwide for its resorts and condominiums and has 155,000 residents and three million visitors a year.

Due to foreign competition in sugar, the hotel closed in 1952. Unable to afford moving his family to the "big city" of Honolulu (then with only 250,000 residents; now the entire Island of Oahu has one million residents), Dad left us (wife Setsuyo and three young sons—I'm the middle one) back on Maui while he searched for a job in Waikiki. He found one as a dining room waiter at the Halekulani Hotel (where he worked until his retirement) and sent for us after saving up for a year. My cousins will never let me forget that, when I came over from Maui, it was the first time I had ever watched TV—and I threw up!

My Mom, Setsuyo, born in the McGerrow sugar plantation camp on Maui, was the oldest daughter of Japanese immigrant contract laborers, who were also from Fukushima Prefecture. After attending school at Puunene through the eighth grade, she was apprenticed as a seamstress. When we moved to Honolulu, she got what turned out to be a career job as an assembly line worker at the Dole Pineapple Cannery (closed in the 1970s, also the result of foreign competition).

With my immigrant and working class background, I often felt like an imposter during my years at Princeton, Yale, and Harvard, as I moved in and around the upper- and middle-class milieu of the Ivy League. Whenever I returned home for the summers—and, eventually, when I came home in the 1970s to settle down permanently—I had to learn to "code-switch" (e.g., speak the Island patois of pidgin English, as appropriate) and to be a chameleon, often having to readjust my go-getter East Coast attitude to the more relaxed Island style. For example, when I first returned to Hawaii to settle down, I was often asked, "How come you walk so fast?"

Lucky Lesson #6

Count your blessings—and try to do something good with them!

I thank God each day for the many blessings bestowed on me. After all, it's not every day (or year) that anyone is blessed enough to earn degrees at Princeton, Yale, and Harvard, in that order—akin to a three-goal hat trick in ice hockey. My own career pattern and predilection (so different from many other individuals with law or MPA degrees) have always been to use my "fancy" advanced degrees and knowledge to help other people.

Yale Law School provided me with that opportunity early on. In the summer of 1966 and spring break of 1967, I worked as a federal inspector and was sent off to the South to ascertain whether local public school districts there were making a bona fide effort to integrate Black children into their pre-school, federally funded Head Start programs. I met with public school officials and with Black parents in neighborhoods in Jena, Louisiana; Milledgeville, Georgia; and Greenville, South Carolina. When you're young, you usually don't think anything bad will happen to you. But looking back, I now realize that, with the Civil Rights Movement in full swing at that time, I could easily have been shot or hanged by racists.

In the mid-1970s, soon after I returned home to Hawaii to settle down permanently, I volunteered to serve as a pro bono

counsel to George Helm, the musician and activist who led the
movement to stop the US military from dropping bombs on the
island of Kahoʻolawe, off the southern coast of Maui. Kahoʻolawe
had been used for target practice ever since it was designated
for that purpose not long after the bombing of Pearl Harbor on
December 7, 1941. Sadly, George disappeared in March 1977—
never to be found—while paddling a surfboard from Kahoʻolawe
toward Maui with his cousin, Kimo Mitchell. Through
copious tears, I wrote the album liner notes for his posthumous
album, "George Helm: A True Hawaiian" (available through
Cord International). I also negotiated an agreement whereby
the military agreed to allow Native Hawaiians once-a-month
access to Kahoʻolawe to practice their pre-missionary religious
rituals. (In 1990, President George H.W. Bush stopped the
bombing permanently. In 1994, the federal government returned
Kahoʻolawe to the State of Hawaii for safekeeping until the Island
becomes the land base for a new revived Nation of Hawaii
within the USA.)

More recently, for 24 years before retiring, I worked as
a professor of business law and criminal justice at a private
independent university, Hawaii Pacific University, encouraging
and mentoring students for their future careers.

Lucky Lesson #7

Not bad for a Princeton flunk-out! I have learned that, with resiliency and faith in God, you can flunk out of Princeton, return like prodigal progeny, and then go on to earn degrees at Yale Law School and Harvard Kennedy School.

I flunked out of Princeton at the end of my sophomore year. I thank God for helping me muster up the resilience to overcome that terrible mistake, and I hope and pray that, should you encounter a setback of such magnitude, you too will, by the grace of God, be able to rebound successfully.

I earned failing grades in three of my five courses during the second term of my sophomore year. I was asked to leave Princeton, to make up my course deficiencies elsewhere (I did so at the University of Hawaii-Manoa), and then to reapply for admission as a first-term junior. Luckily for me, Princeton follows the philosophy with prodigal progeny that, if it accepts you as a freshman in the first place, it assumes that you can do four years of adequate academic work and earn your bachelor's degree— whenever that may be.

Why did I "crash out" of Princeton? I got "too big for my britches." I had been the editor-in-chief of the student newspaper at Roosevelt High School and had also edited, through my senior year, the weekly youth section of the (now-defunct)

Honolulu Advertiser. Then I worked as a full-time reporter for the *Advertiser*—both before leaving for Princeton and between my freshman and sophomore years there. When I got to Princeton, I successfully entered the writing competition to become a reporter for the student newspaper, the *Daily Princetonian.* Unfortunately, however, as I became a "star" reporter for the newspaper, I began to view this extracurricular work—and not my academic courses—as my primary role, and my grades began to slip.

All of this came to a head in February 1962, when I was chosen out of the entire reportorial staff to go down to Cape Canaveral and cover the US space program's first circumnavigation of the Earth by astronaut John Glenn. I witnessed the blastoff and filed my dispatches from Cocoa Beach, Florida, but, when I got back to Princeton, I completely neglected my studies and flunked three of my five courses. How devastating and depressing!

It was only through a lot of prayer and a lot of hard work that I was able—in my year away from Princeton between my sophomore and junior years—to find the resilience to bounce back from this awful mistake. I was lucky to get a job during my "year off" as a full-time reporter for the *Honolulu Advertiser,* covering the police beat and then the State of Hawaii legislature.

When I was readmitted to Princeton and started my junior year, I was determined not to mess up again. Aside from attending classes, I practically lived in the University library, studying there every evening until it closed at midnight. My effort paid off: I was able to ace all of my courses in my junior and senior years. And my grade point average was so high that I missed making Phi Beta Kappa—the top 10 percent of the graduating class—by only two spots. I took that as a sign that this was my much-deserved punishment for flunking out!

Afterword

These are the Lucky 7 Lessons that I gleaned, outside the classrooms, at Princeton, Yale, and Harvard. Put yourself in my shoes: Would you have learned similar lessons? Everyone is unique. I wouldn't be surprised if—from your own unique higher education experiences outside the classroom—you have your very own set of Lucky 7 Lessons!

Sincerely and Aloha from Hawaii,
Melvin (Mel) Masuda

CPSIA information can be obtained
at www.ICGtesting.com
Printed in the USA
BVHW040821021021
617912BV00012BA/211